Viola Book

One

by Cassia Harvey

CHP295

©2015 by C. Harvey Publications All Rights Reserved.
6403 N. 6th Street
Philadelphia, PA 19126
www.charveypublications.com

1. A, B, and C#

Cassia Harvey

2. The Ladybug: A Hungarian Folk Song

©2015 C. Harvey Publications All Rights Reserved.

3. A, B, C#, and D

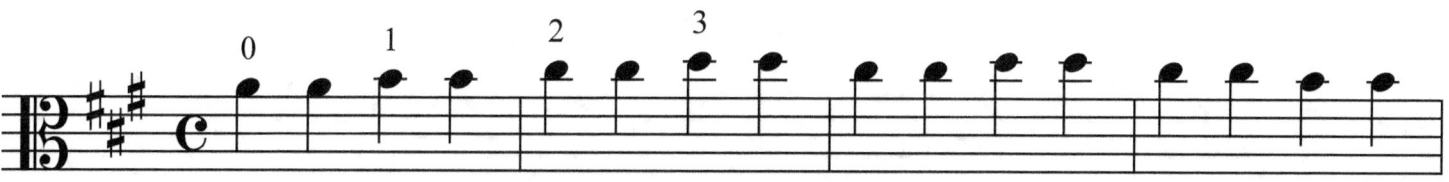

Half Notes get 2 counts!

4. By Our Gates: A Russian Folk Song

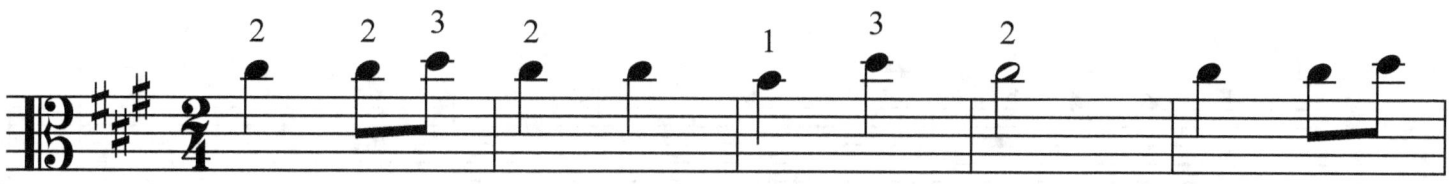

5. Skipping Around the A-String Notes

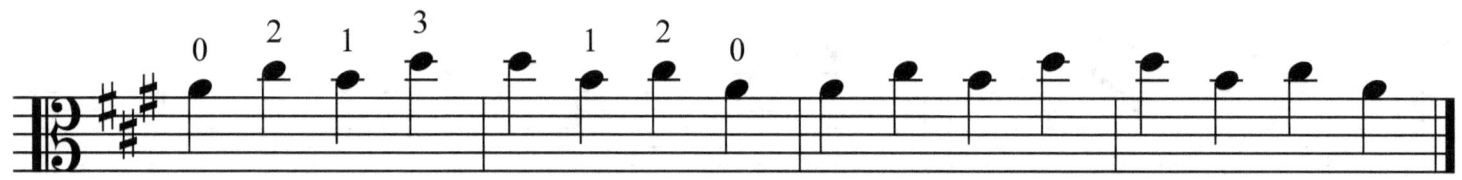

6. Contredanse: A Danish Folk Song

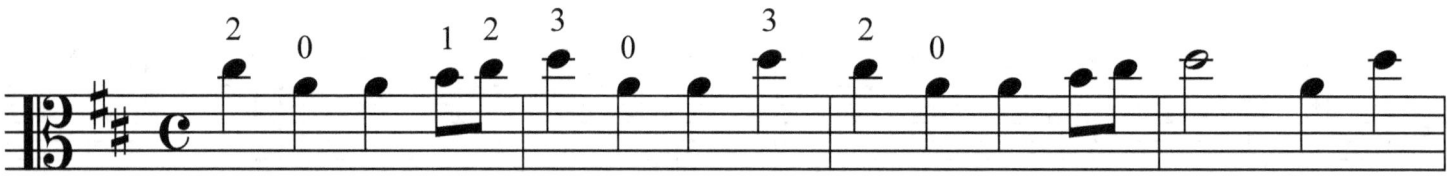
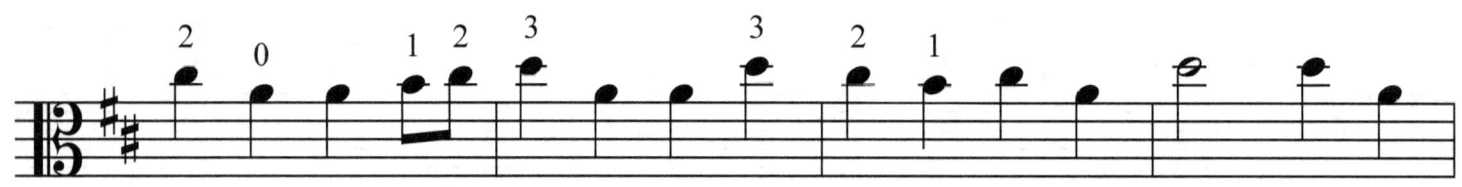
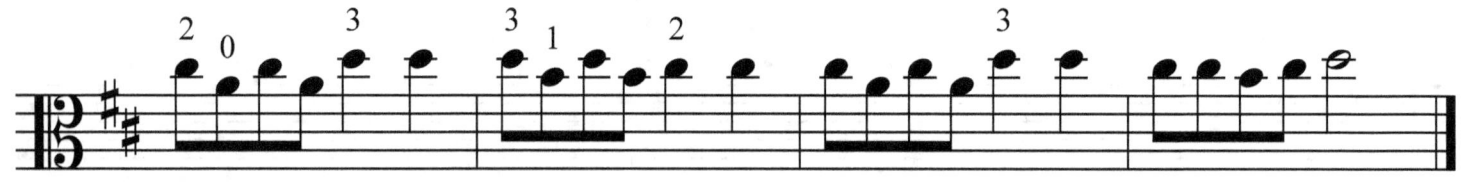

©2015 C. Harvey Publications All Rights Reserved.

7. Learning 4th Finger E

8. Fiddle Tune

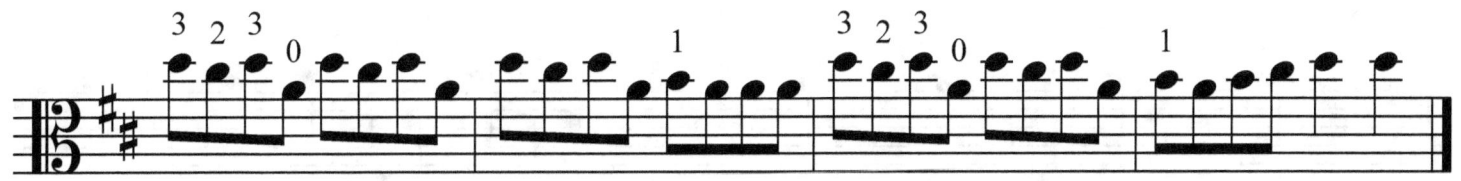

9. Finger Training on D and A

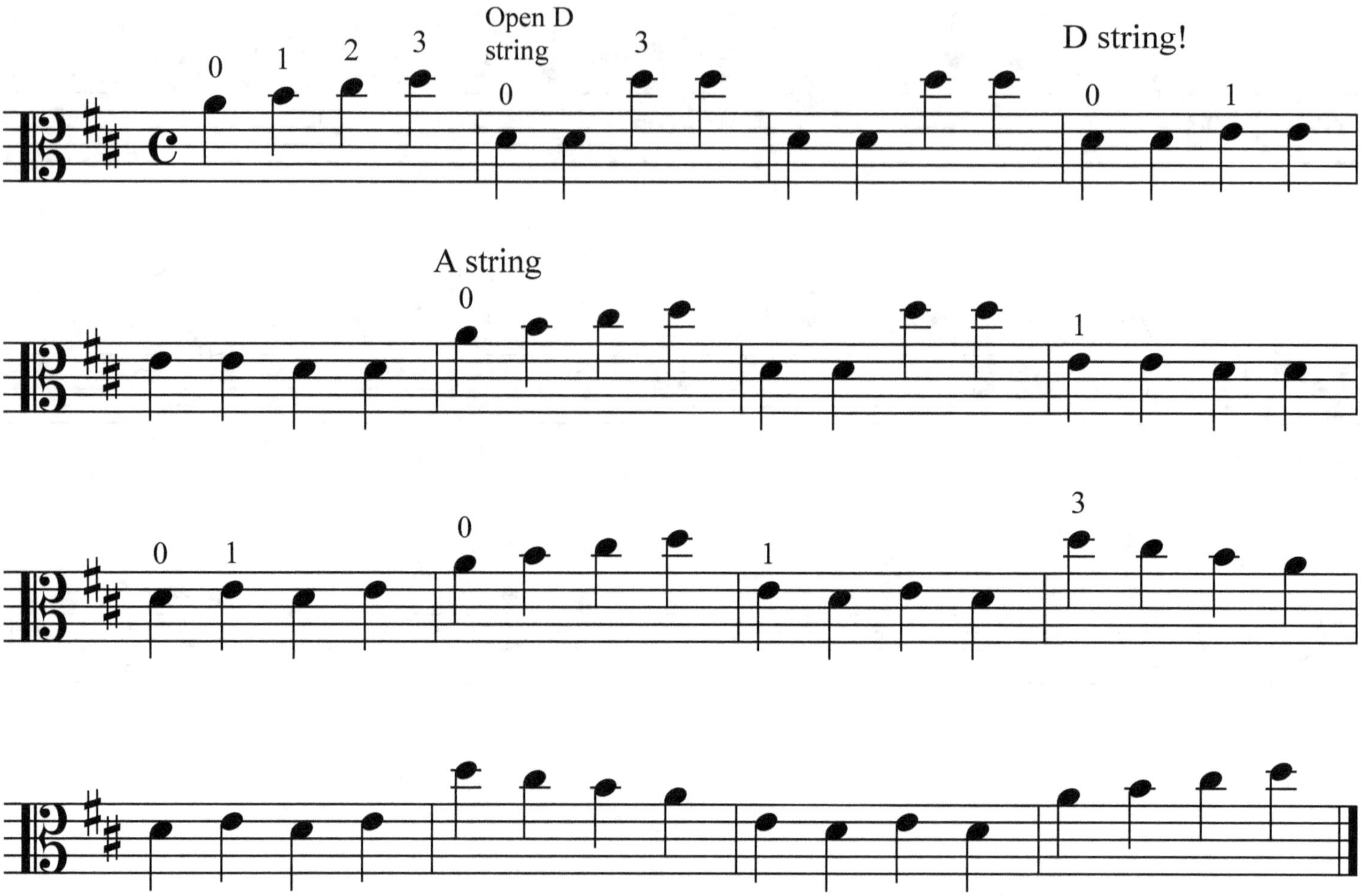

10. String Crossing

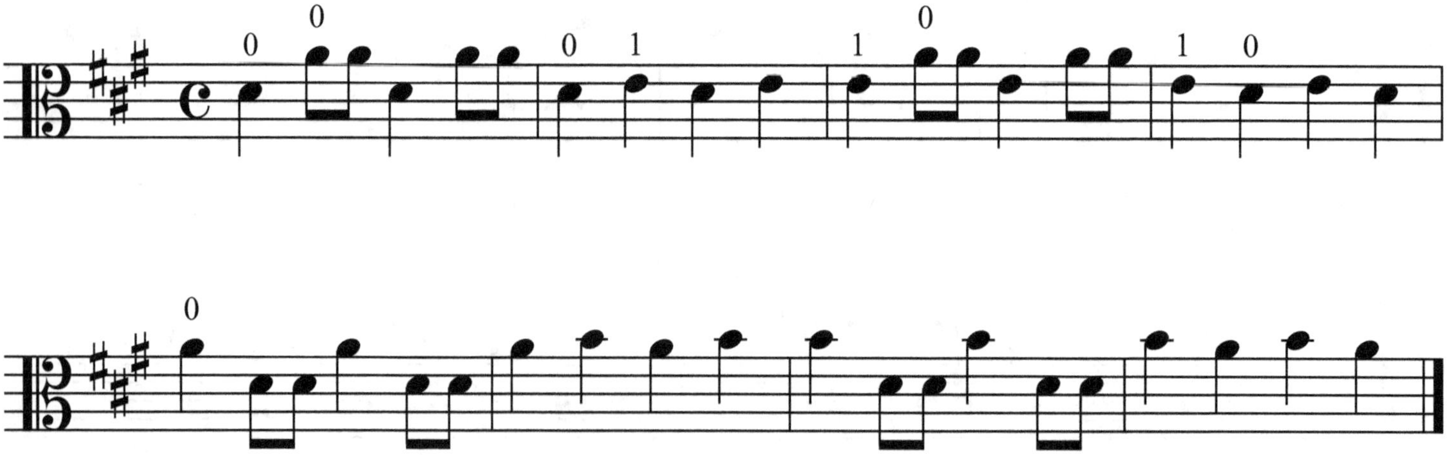

©2015 C. Harvey Publications All Rights Reserved.

11. March

12. Polly Wolly Doodle: An American Folk Song

13. More notes on the D string

14. Crossing to the D string

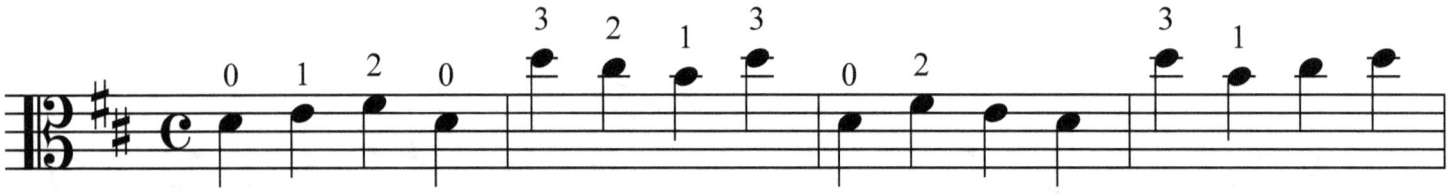

15. The Bold Soldier: A Traditional Folk Song

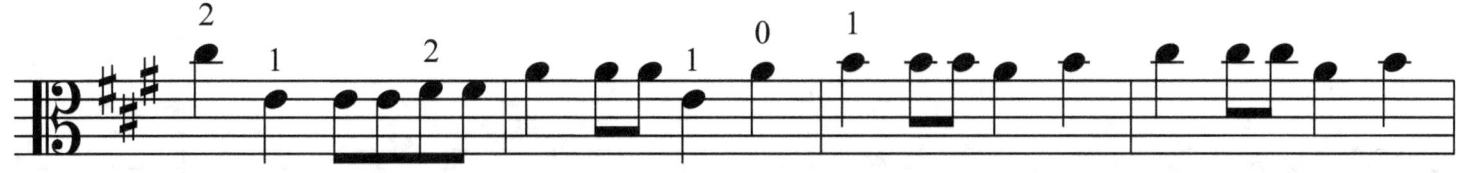

16. Johnny's Gone for a Soldier: An American Folk Song
(play 2 times)

©2015 C. Harvey Publications All Rights Reserved.

17. Finger Workout on A and D

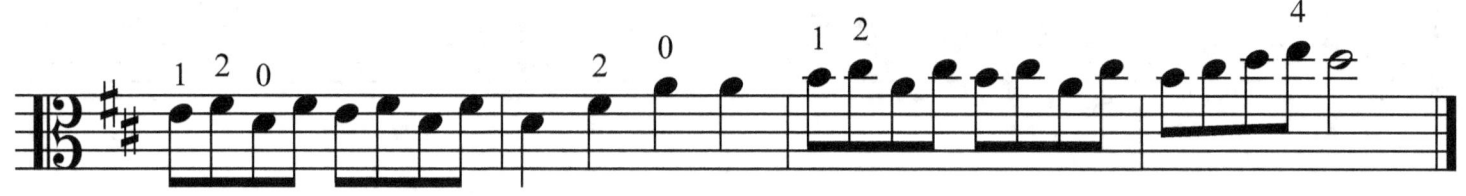

18. 4th Finger on the D string

19. Jasmine Flower: A Chinese Folk Song

20. Tibetan Dance

Dotted half notes get 3 counts!

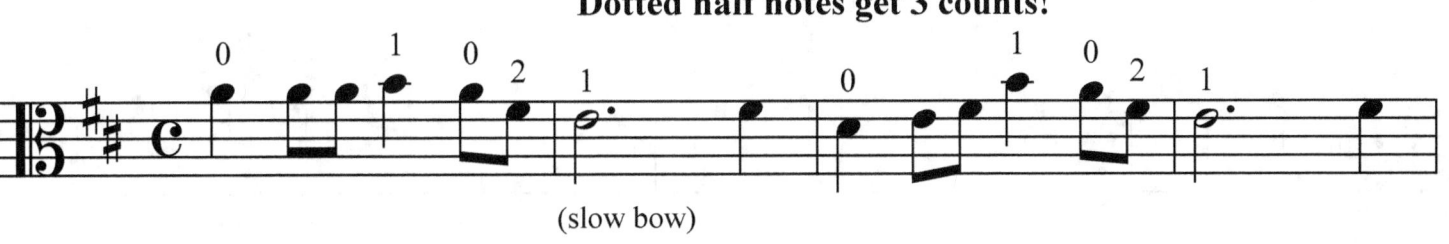

(slow bow)

21. Playing Fourth Finger A

22. Crossing Strings

Viola Book One

23. Crowninshield's Mother Goose

©2015 C. Harvey Publications All Rights Reserved.

24. Crossing Strings and Skipping Notes

25. Bowing Practice

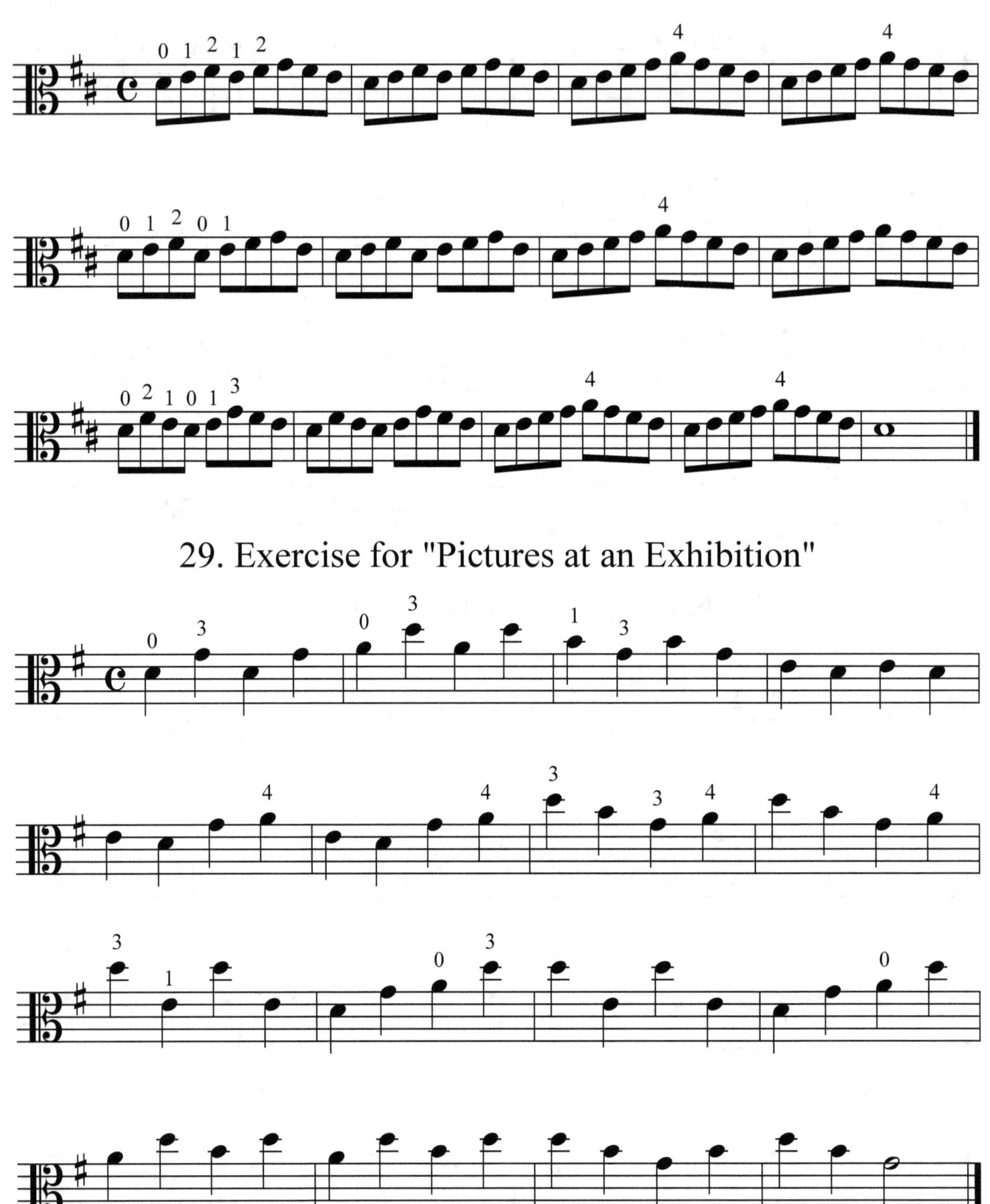

Viola Book One

30. Waltz by Alexandrov

31. Theme from Mussorgsky's "Pictures at an Exhibition"

©2015 C. Harvey Publications All Rights Reserved.

32. Low Second Finger C♮

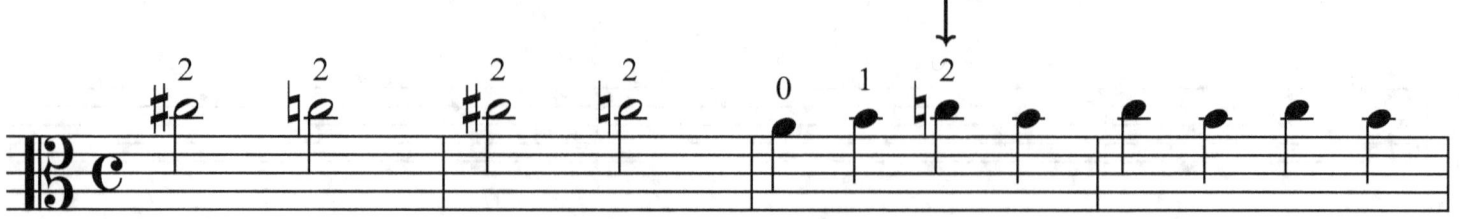

33. Low Second Finger F♮

34. Spanish Minuet

35. Donizetti's Theme from L'Elisir D'Amor

©2015 C. Harvey Publications All Rights Reserved.

36. High and Low 2nd Finger

37. Third Finger on D: There is an F# in the Key Signature!

38. Second Finger on the G String

Viola Book One

39. Dance from Tchaikovsky's Swan Lake

©2015 C. Harvey Publications All Rights Reserved.

40. The Notes on the G string

41. Crossing Over to the G String

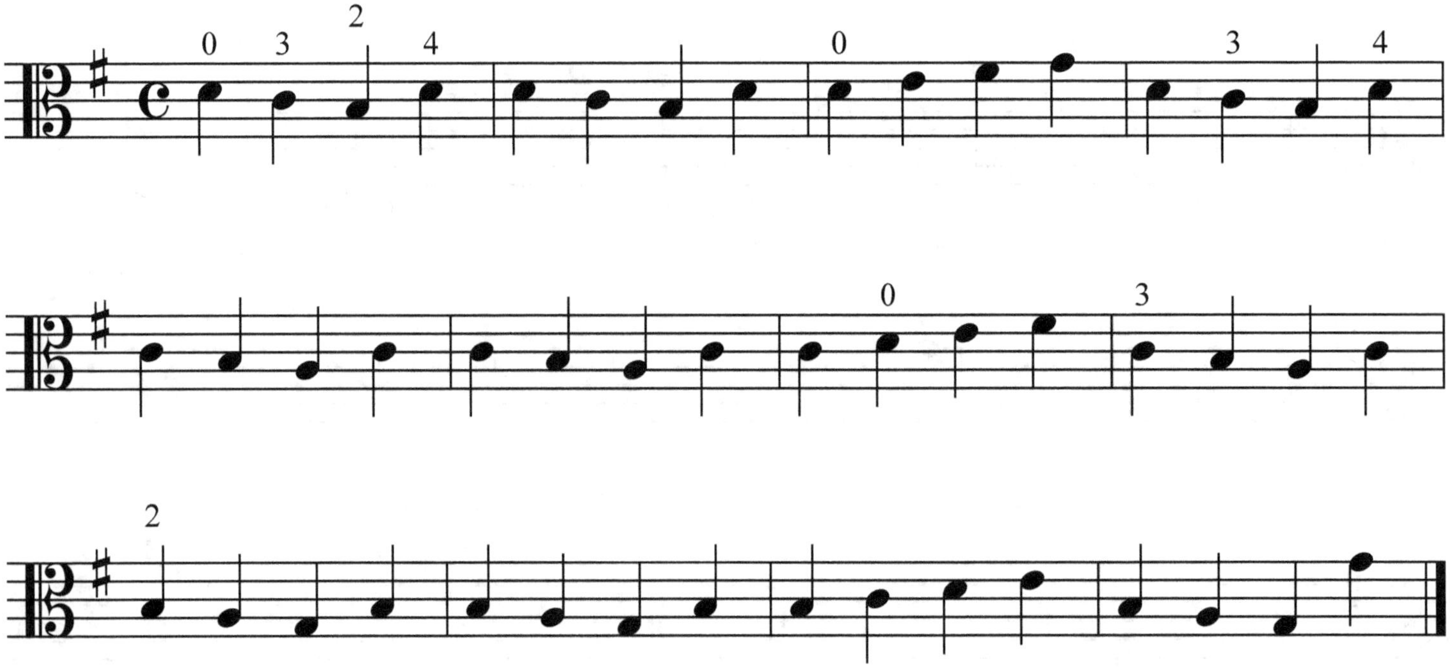

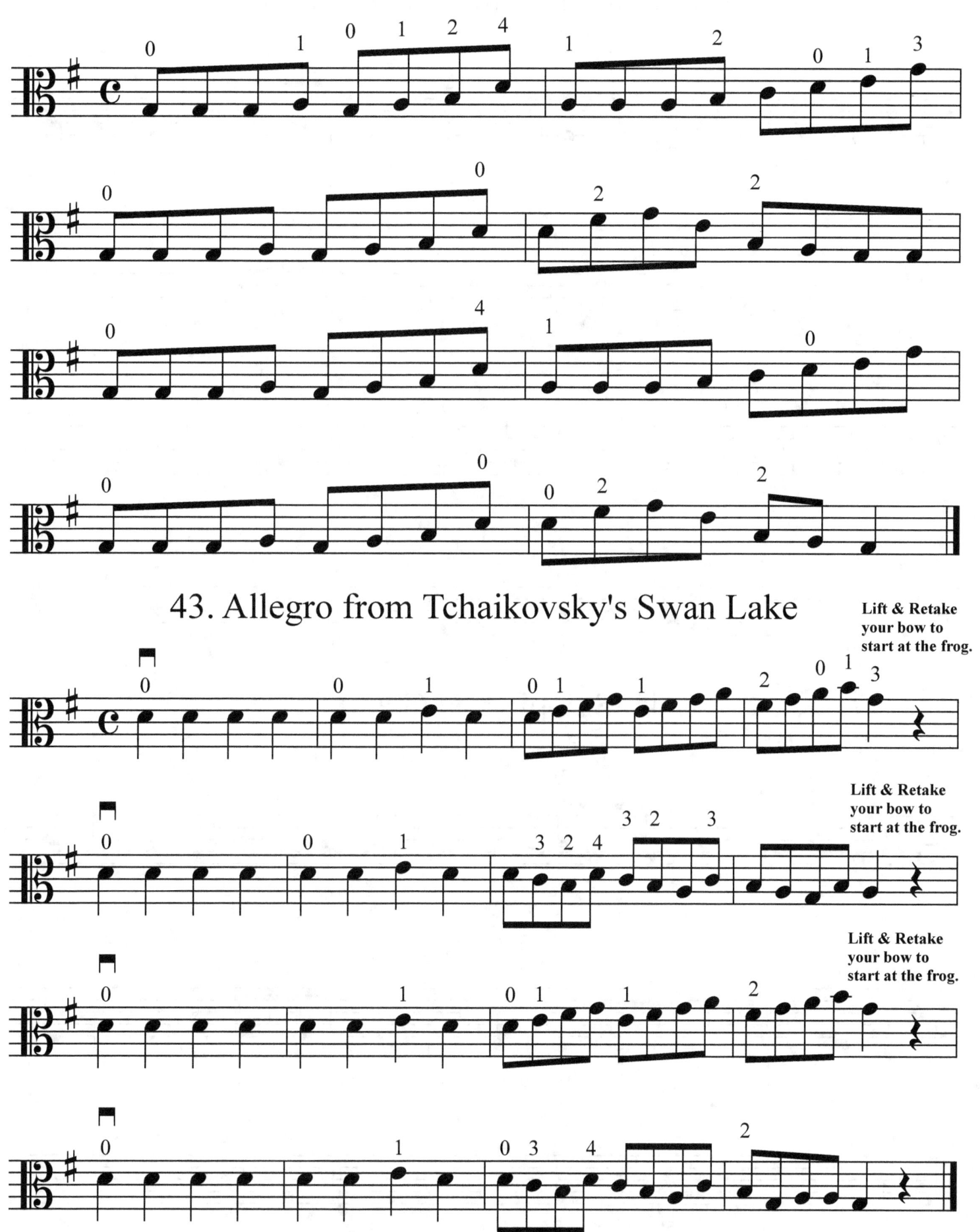

44. The Notes on the G and C strings

45. Skipping on G and C

Viola Book One

46. Theme from Rimsky-Korsakov's Scheherazade

47. Ballet Music from Schubert's Rosamunde

©2015 C. Harvey Publications All Rights Reserved.

48. High and Low 2nd Finger

49. Review Exercise

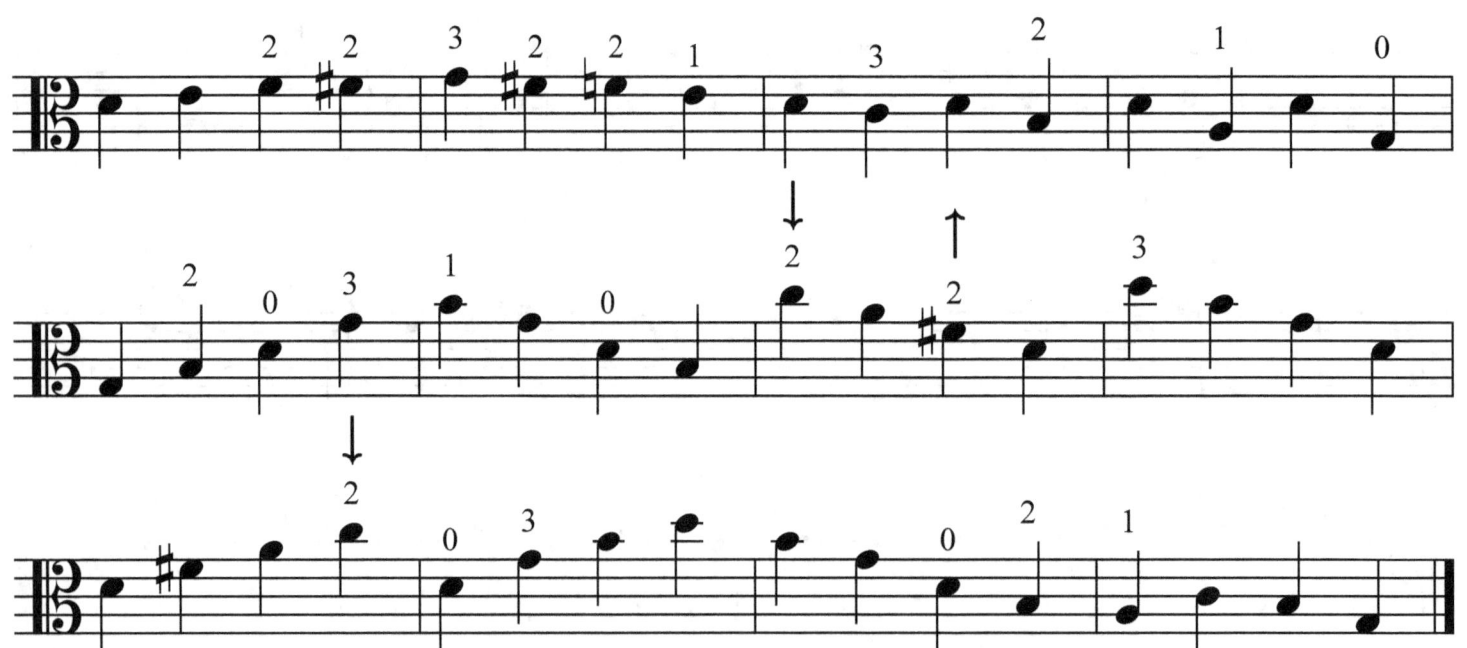

50. Theme from Mahler's First Symphony

51. Galopade, by Glinka

52. Sliding Back to Low 1st Finger

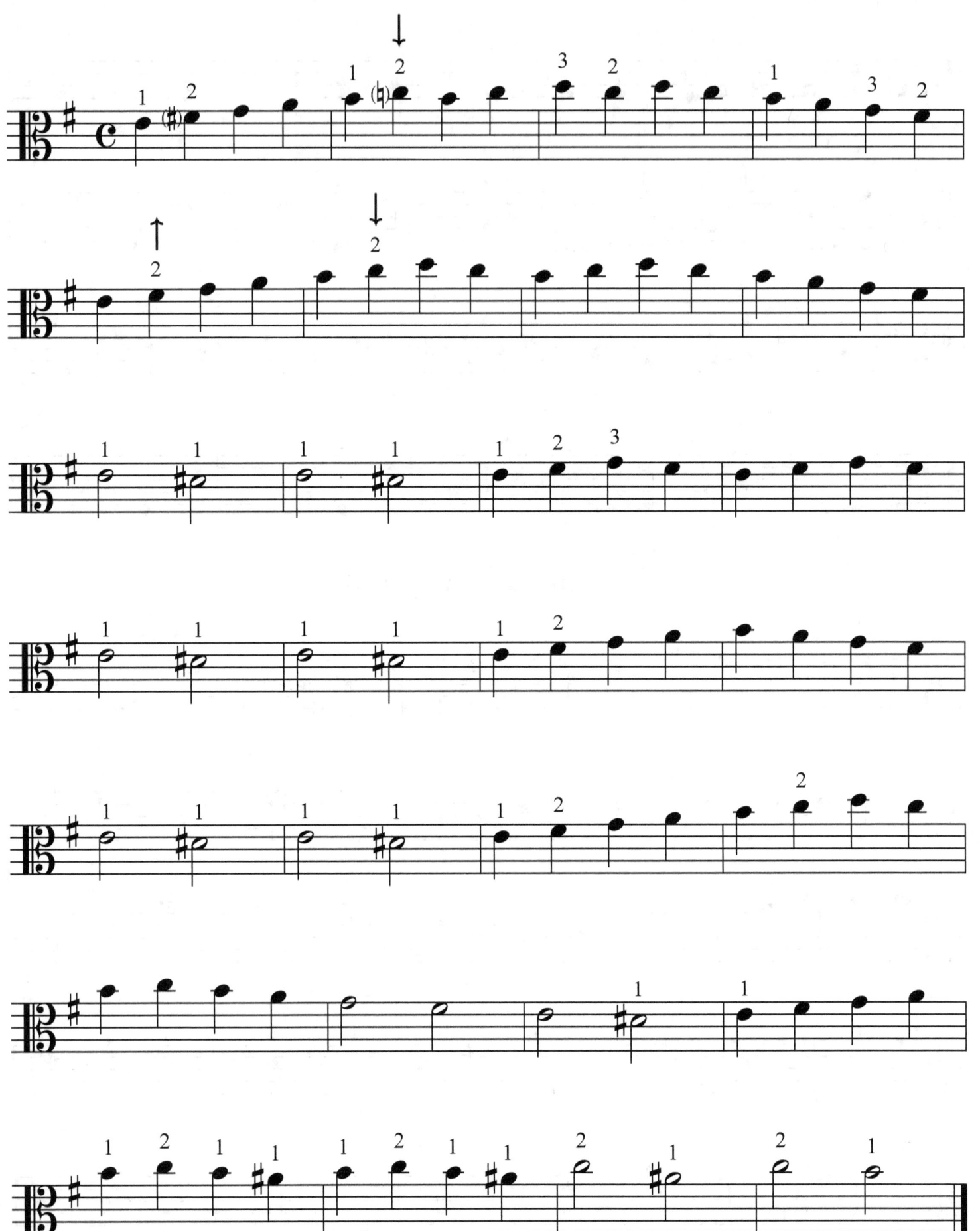

53. I Went to Sea for Oranges: A Spanish Folk Song

54. Mozart's Alleluia

55. Reaching Across to High 3rd Finger

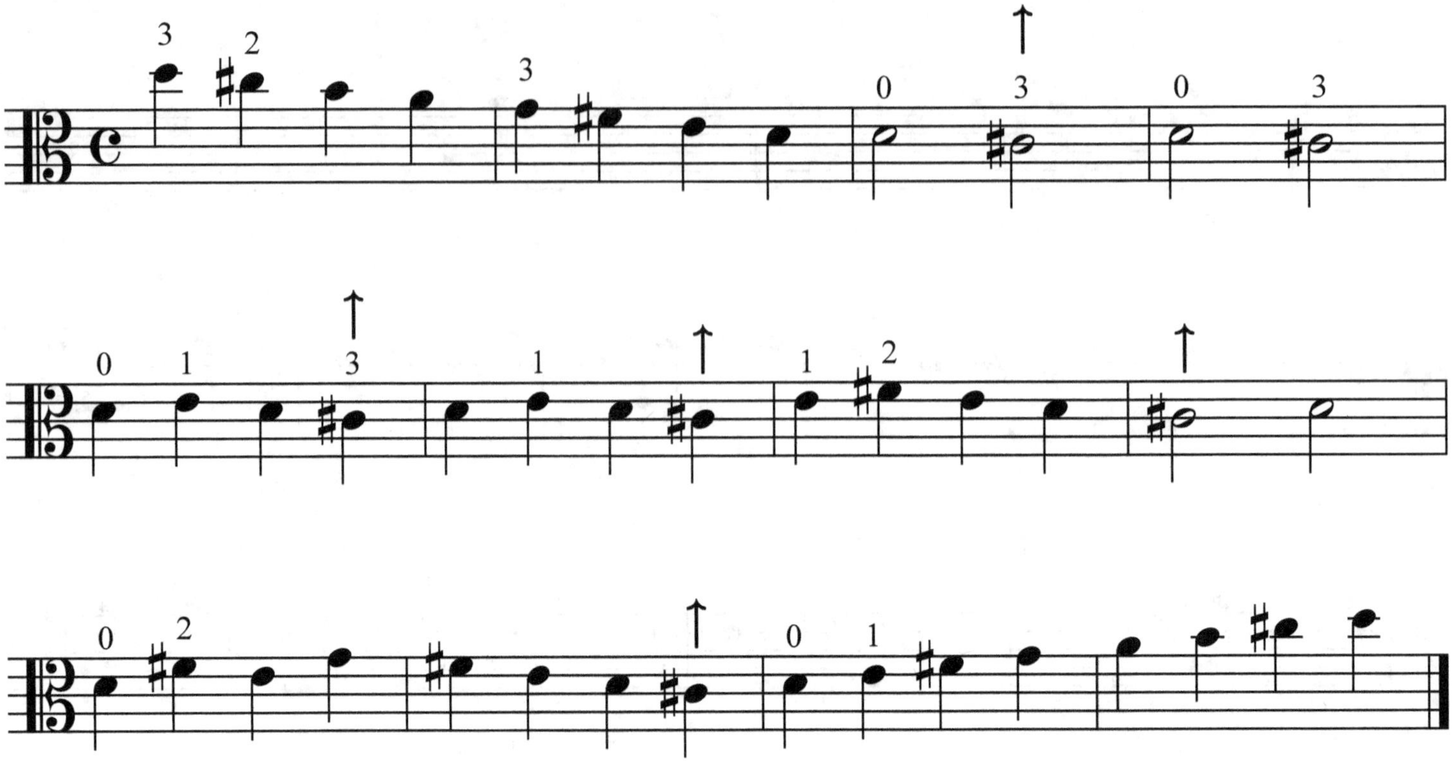

56. Sliding to and from High 3rd Finger

available from www.charveypublications.com:

CHP133
Knowing the Notes for Viola

The Note D; open string

Cassia Harvey

©2005 C. Harvey Publications All Rights Reserved.

www.ingramcontent.com/pod-product-compliance
Lightning Source LLC
Chambersburg PA
CBHW051430070526
44584CB00023B/3664